There is a sticker for every page.
Answer the question and find
the right sticker.

British Library Cataloguing in Publication Data
for this book are available from the British Library.

ISBN 0-86163-911-1(paperback)

Published by Award Publications Limited,
1st Floor, 27 Longford Street
London NW1 3DZ

Printed in China

The Children's Book of Manners

Sue Lloyd

Illustrated by

Jaqueline East

AWARD PUBLICATIONS LIMITED

Not waiting for your turn

The children love the slide. But they are not waiting for their turn. Look how they push and shove. No one can get on the slide. Tom has hurt his knee.

Who has hurt his knee?

The children love the slide. They are waiting for their turn. Look at their wiggly line. Now everyone can get on the slide. Tom is waving from the top.

Do you wait for your turn?

Sam wants to share his sweets with the other children. Greedy Dan wants them all for himself. He stuffs the sweets into his mouth. He does not say 'thank you' to Sam.

Who wants all the sweets?

Sam shares his sweets with everyone. The children take one each. They all say 'thank you'. Josh takes a toffee. Lizzy takes a gobstopper. James and Poppy take pear drops. Delicious!

Do you say 'thank you'?

Sally is standing all by herself. She feels sad and lonely. The children are whispering and pointing at her. No one will play with her or be her friend. Except Toffo.

Who is Sally's friend?

Sally looks happy now. She does not feel sad or lonely. The children want to play ball with her. They will all be friends together. But Sally's best friend will be Toffo.

Have you been kind today?

Not sharing

It is playtime. The children want to go in the playhouse. But Katie got there first. She will not share the toys. She keeps them all for herself. "Go away," she says.

Who keeps the toys for herself?

It is lunchtime. Katie is sharing the playhouse with the other children. They are all playing together. Katie thinks it is more fun to share. "Come in," she says.

Do you share your toys?

"Stop!" shouts Mum. But it is too late. James,Tom, and Toffo leave mud on the carpet, on the stairs, and even on the walls. There is mud everywhere.

Who shouts 'stop'?

This time the children hang up their coats. They leave their muddy boots on the door mat. Tom dries Toffo with a towel. It is good fun. Mum and Dad are very pleased.

Are you clean indoors?

Not tidying your room

Jack cannot find his favourite toy. His bedroom is so untidy. Dad is very cross.

Jack's clothes and toys are lying everywhere. He is looking for Kylie the koala.

Who is looking for Kylie?

There is Kylie in the cupboard. Jack has tidied his bedroom. Dad is very pleased. Now Jack can find all of his toys when he wants to play with them.

Do you tidy your bedroom?

"Be careful, Poppy!" cries Mum. But Poppy is not careful. She spills her soup over Mum. Josh will not turn round. Megan pours her soup into her mouth. No one enjoys their dinner.

Who spills her soup over Mum?

I was kind today
I say 'thank you'
Toffo
Poppy
Crumble
Katie
I have good manners
Sam
Mum
Josh
Meena
Jack
Tom
Mrs Batty

Tom

I wait for
my turn

Dan

I tidy my
bedroom

I share
my toys

I am clean
indoors

I
was
quiet
today

Toffo

I
say
'please'

I put
litter in
the bin

I listen at
story-time

I say
'sorry'

I hold the
door open

I play
safely

The children sit quietly. They are waiting for Mum to cut the cake. It is Poppy's favourite. Josh and Megan like it, too. So does Toffo. Everyone enjoys their pudding.

Do you have good manners?

Not saying 'sorry'

Crash! Mum's favourite vase is smashed. Tom knocked it over. But he does not stop to say 'sorry'. He is too busy playing ball with Toffo. Mum is very upset.

Who is Tom playing with?

Tom smashed Mum's favourite vase. Mum is crying. Tom is crying, too. "Sorry," he says, "it was an accident." He hopes they can glue the pieces back together.

Do you say 'sorry'?

Dad has got a bad cold. But the children do not care. Bang! Bang! Josh bangs the drum. Poppy shouts and the baby wakes up. Poor Dad feels even worse.

Who bangs the drum?

The children are being quiet because Dad has got a bad cold. They turn the television off. Poppy is reading to Josh.
The baby is sleeping quietly.
Dad is feeling much better.

Were you quiet today?

"Give me my present!" yells Tom. He is very rude. He stamps his foot and shouts at Santa. Tom will not say 'please', so Santa will not give him a Christmas present.

Who shouts at Santa?

"Please may I have a present, Santa?" asks Tom. He is very excited. Santa gives him a present. What is inside the box? Tom hopes it will be a toy car.

Do you say 'please'?

Not putting litter in the bin

Lizzy and James do not like this street. There is litter everywhere – on the pavement, in the gutter, and even in the tree. Crumble has cut her paw on the broken glass.

Who has cut her paw?

Lizzy and James like this street. It is clean and tidy. The children put their litter in the bin. Toffo helps them. This street is safe for everyone, even for cats.

Do you put litter in the bin?

Not listening at story-time

It is story-time, but what a noise! Poppy and Tom are talking. Meena is tickling her friend. Sam is doing a handstand. Mrs Batty is losing her glasses. No one can hear the story.

Who is doing a handstand?

Look at the children now. They are listening to the story. Mrs Batty shows them a funny picture. It makes the children laugh. Now everyone can hear the story.

Do you listen at story-time?

Not holding the door open

"Meena!" calls Jack. "Please hold the door open." But it is too late. Meena slams the door so the children bump into each other. Their instruments fly everywhere.

Who slams the door?

"Thank you, Meena," says Jack. Meena holds the door open for the other children. They can all walk safely to their music lessons. Toffo feels safest in Poppy's bag!

Do you hold the door open?

Where is Poppy? She was here a minute ago. Mrs Batty is very worried. The children are worried too. They are looking everywhere. Where can Poppy be?

Who is very worried?

There she is. Poppy is flying her kite in the field. She is safe. Mrs Batty tells Poppy to stay with the other children.
She must never run off on her own.

Do you play safely?